FACILITATION OF WILL POWER

FACILITATION OF WILL POWER

Dr. Yvonne Luk

PARTRIDGE

Library of Congress Control Number:		2015957723
ISBN:	Softcover	978-1-4828-5461-9
	eBook	978-1-4828-5462-6

Because of the dynamic nature of the Internet, any web addresses or links contained in this book may have changed since publication and may no longer be valid. The views expressed in this work are solely those of the author and do not necessarily reflect the views of the publisher, and the publisher hereby disclaims any responsibility for them.

Print information available on the last page.

To order additional copies of this book, contact
Toll Free 800 101 2657 (Singapore)
Toll Free 1 800 81 7340 (Malaysia)
orders.singapore@partridgepublishing.com

www.partridgepublishing.com/singapore

Contents

In memory of my loving mother Alice Leung who inspired my writing and working effort, to my father Francis Chan who was always by my side whenever I needed his opinions. This book is also dedicated to my husband Paul Luk, my daughter Dorothy, my son-in-law Andrew Brown, my granddaughter Victoria, whom they have been acting very supportively on my life-time goal from England.

Preface

I started a job in nexus to children psychology in 1970 which was my first teaching job in a nursery and preparatory school right after my graduation from English and commercial school at the age of 17. The small kids in my class were all came from poverty class, not every one of them shared similar intellectual learning behaviour, some of them had speech deficits, even some showed a certain degree of autism disorder characterized by aggression. Since the preparatory school was a charity funded school, it was opened to children whose parents were refugees fled from mainland China where this school was located in the area of public housing built and provided by the British Government to settle them in Hong Kong. I met a lot of problems coping with difficult kids in my class, communicating with their parents to understand their difficult children was even impossible because of language barrier, they responded my concern with just a laugh or smile and then turned away to bring their children home after school hour, at first I viewed they were just rejecting my enquiries, but after few attempts to make them speak with me I realized these parents avoided to discuss their children problems with me was due to their low educational standard from mainland China, for whom they had gone through a revolution turmoil that even they themselves were cognitive dysfunction, this became really a headache problem for me to cope with their troublesome children.

Within the first two months of my job I suffered insomnia and cried a lot for facing the problems in teaching difficult children who created trouble every minute in the class, but thanks to the help of my dearest mother who had twenty years of experience in teaching career, that she began to discuss with me on the topics of understanding and helping students at small age with abnormal behaviour. She listened to my problems very patiently and spent almost two hours to correct my inexperienced teaching flaws to cope with the fear I was facing with innovative attitude to solve and guide the chaos of my work every night before bed time. One day the principal who ran the preparatory and who was a catholic nun called us in her office to inform all teaching staff that a course in Children Psychology For Kindergarden Teachers was organized for us to take. In the first lesson of the course the lecturer emphasized specifically on the importance of training the students' hand muscles on holding a pencil firmly and steadily in right position, and to observe their fingers movement to putative the measures of their brain development which was really a very interested for the start of learning, gradually I became interested in taking neuropsychology. At the end of the school term I was very happy that the kids were taken into famous primary school education, all my hardship was paid off. After gaining a year of teaching experience from preparatory school, I took another job in teaching young junior school students in basis of Children Psychology for Teaching, the mastery of techniques in prominent teaching profiles propelled my effort to contribute the target result, and as a propulsion for my continuation in learning psychology by engaging with part-time distance course, part-time day release course and the External Courses of The University Of Hong Kong to brush up my teaching effort in children psychology. After a year the principal of the school gave me a promotion to teach the graduation English classes. In 1972, a catholic American nun who was a coworker of my mother in the past offered me a place in their hospital to establish a formal Volunteer Department for training youth development in compliance with The Duke Of Edinburg Award Scheme. In my job, my responsibility was to help them to understand the psychological needs of the sick in the hospital, and by assigning them to work in the nursery, pharmacy, and library, they learnt to set up goals for their future by interacting with medical staff and with nurses, through working with them, they were being trained to seek social values and insight to form social behaviour as they were preparing to graduate from high school in a year time, they will become an asset by the training pattern to develop their personality leading to good social adjustment. In 1973 under my mother's influenced of being passionate in helping needy people in the church, I decided to join the convent, but departed in 1975 after being a novice and working with them in one of their school of discovering at last convent life did not fit me. My father Francis who always encouraged me to take a wider scope of life in order to protract my success with more opportunities, he did not agree I was just working in an area with only children and teenage which could not fabricate a unique perspective and confidence for my goal, he then recommended me to work in his civil engineering construction company as his assistant to gain further experience for my life. I insisted to stand on my own two feet to make the opportunity by myself rather than under his shadow and started my secretarial administration work in business firms. Besides gaining working experiences, becoming mature through coping difficulties with team work was one of the greatest achievements which benefit my wisdom as growing older. In the year 1980 The Social Work Department invited me to engage with their rehabilitation program of setting up a rehabilitation center and hostel for the transition of the released prisoners in murdering cases by impulsive behaviour of mental disorder, and were sentenced to prison for 25 years, as well as providing the psychological support to the juvenile delinquencies during the period of legal trials from the court, my role was to reeducate their behaviour and motivate their drive in occupational training for returning back to normal society. My targets to reeducate them was running on Adler's system of the three major tasks of work, friendship, loving care among their friendship to help each other since their own family had abandoned and left them. The training included coping life problems by self-control for being responsible of their future, helping them to understand occupational task required cooperation, personal courage to be willing to contribute the welfare of others in their job, socialization and interaction with normal citizens. My decision to retake Psychology was made by the imperishable effort I helped the released prisoners and adolescent with recognition, I took part-time in external study in The University Of Hong Kong in 1984 for Organization Psychology and Personnel Management to start my decision, and continued in 1993 for Social Science and Social Psychology in The Open University, in 1996 I was offered credits transferred by The University Of Queensland for a continuation of PhD Program Degree. In those ten years I made my practice in the fields of autism disorder, learning difficulty, and in Cognitive Behavioural and Psychotherapy which I spent my practice and training in Brisbane and Melbourn in 2003 and in 2004 to complete the degree.

Maturity and wisdom means never give up every moment we experience in life, even grasping hold of the failure as an experience to transform the flaws into energy for making success. Working in the business sector I gained the experience of regenerating behaviour (e.g. will power, competent), and those from the clients I learnt the assumption of objectivity on psychosocial growth, I wish to share these experiences with the readers of my books as part of my work to help others coping meander of their life.

death they may be associating with, because acute stress can possibly aggravate cardiovascular disease. Rozanski, Blumenthal, and Kaplan (1999) note, acute stress can cause constriction of the coronary arteries, arrhythmias in the heartbeat, stimulation of platelet function (which promotes the formation of clots), and increased viscosity of the blood.

In 2003, I was assigned to treat a group of volunteers in a non-profitable organization facing with infectious SARS disease after they had offered their visiting service to the in-patient wards, which every one of the volunteers suffered from insomnia, emotional problems, and eating disorders underlined health problems. The method which I applied was DBT (Dialectic Behaviour Therapy) for group therapy; the goal was to train these patients to learn coping response, so that they are able to exert certain control over an aversive situation that can reduce their stressful situation. Within the CBT, I had to observe the selective abstraction of the patients whom they misunderstood their continuation for success were deprived, and DBT is my goal to encourage them to create "a meaningful life fulfilled with values of worth. Three weeks later these patients reported that they regained appetite, they began to re-build trust in life and family relationships without fear of infecting their love ones, and even some recovered from recurrence of upper respiratory infection. From these studies, I believed stressful situation suppressed immune system, to further explain stress increases the secretion of glucocorticoids. Stone et al. (1982) suggest that the effect is caused by decreased production of a particular immunoglobulin that present in the secretions of mucous membranes, including those in the nose, mouth, throat, and lungs. The immunoglobulin, IgA, serves as the first defense against infectious microorganisms that enter the nose or mouth. They found that IgA is associated with mood; when a subject is unhappy or depressed, IgA levels are lower than normal. The results suggest that the stress caused by undesirable events may, by suppressing the production of IgA, lead to a rise in the likelihood of upper respiratory infections (Neil R. Carlson).

When patients with chronic illnesses or terminal diseases facing death and approaching to dying, they are likely to suffer from endocrine disease, because the neurotransmitter system interacts with neuromodulators is being disturbed by emotion problems. Norepinephrine and dopamine are the neuromodulators function by the hypothalamus. During the threats to health, patients will experience mood swings for suffering of insomnia followed with anxiety, and therefore the levels of serotonia become low in relating to other neurotransmitters, such as norepinephrine, and dopamine to run the brain circuit in the hypothalamus through the pituitary gland, and couldn't coordinate normally with the endocrine system. Why does anxiety exist during illness? When patients are comprehended by the threatening of painful therapy or in face of terminal stage of their life, their mood-state will then be marked by negative affect, such as bodily respond of tension and apprehension about their future and the small ones in their family. Fear and panic attack are also associated as an abrupt acute discomfort accompanied by physical symptoms of heart palpitations by increases in muscle tension (frontalis EMG) and figure temperature, dizziness, shortness of breath and chest pain. In physiological studies, the sympathetic and parasympathetic divisions of the ANS operate in complimentary fashions, while the SNS is primarily responsible for mobilizing the activities of the glands, allowing oxygen to enter the blood and brain. Brain connection is the major function of emotion and behaviour, by integrating with other areas of the nervous system hypothalamus as in control of the heart rate, elevating blood pressure, as well as the peristaltic activity of the gastrointestinal tract without normal oxygen flow, loss of concentration is one of symptom in panic attack, especially to chronic and terminal illness patients, because of the anxiety associates with depression and mood swing, patients become unable to concentrate on things like reading and normal conversion for so much energy is taken up concentrating on bodily feelings. Panic attack is one of the psychological disorders involve with the hypothalamus and the endocrine system activating by the HYPAC axis that makes primates susceptible to stress, as a result of learned helplessness of which the chronic and terminal illnesses patients have no control over the physical diseases they experience. As Martin Seligman describes people make an attribution that they have no control and become depressed.

Most patients with chronic or terminal diseases are often associated with negative feelings of mood by unfinished business in their life, these are all natural to run in their mind, but these are also depressive automatic thoughts to disturb not merely the patients' mind, also to bring harm to physical health as well, such as circadian rhythm disruption for any emotional loading will erupt the normal homologus functioning of the cerebrospinal fluid. Nausea increasing of pulse rate and vomiting are the symptoms that illustrates unstable flow of the cerebrospinal fluid during panic shocking and depressive moments. Cognitive therapy can work to explain the deep-seated automatic thoughts, and directs the patients' families to understand their worth in life. Methods include correcting negative errors and regaining more realistic thoughts and appraisals. Socrates theory remarked: If one knows what justice is, one acts justly. Thus, cognitive theory in this term conveys the message of positive mind to remedy the errors of self-punishment thoughts that disrupt a normal behaviour. Socratic approach applies a chain to cognitive therapy that definitions are important to rule accurate communication as a guide line for therapeutic techniques and skills. Cognitive therapy is a role of formulating teaching effort for which Socrates believed truth could be shared, and for him the goal is the essence of sharing the truth for formulating knowledge to correct mental errors. In other words CBT is a behaviour training and learning. According to the present psychotherapists Weissman & Markowitz they focuses on resolving problems in existing relationships and learning to form new interpersonal relationships. Following the process of CBT, IPT is applied to deal with mental conflict, regulating the loss of relationship to let-go the grief and finally Identifying and remedying deficits and acquiring new relationship, establishing professional goals, or fulfilling the worth for unfinished business before facing death and dying.

Anxiety in chronic illness and terminal illness trigger potential danger signals to higher cortical processes which Gray & McNaughton call the BIS system. Panic attacks occur when patients are put under each type of medical tests or radiotherapy for cancer, as well as going through the difficult part of chemotherapy, FFS (fight/ flight) system will take place. This is believed that FFS is activated in the raphe nucleus through the amygdala, the ventromedial nucleus of the hypothalamus by deficiencies in serotonin. People are in anxiety and depression for most of the reasons that they suffer serious illness in chronicle diseases. They are in fear of lacking the physical condition like normal others to fulfill their expectations for surviving to achieve self-esteem in life. When the laboratory results place them in vulnerable mind, they will start questioning about the values of life for what purpose they were born to suffer and become a burden of their family, they doubt that the world they live in has become meaningless which are only occupied with schedules of clinical appointments, medications and treatments, pain in their body which they suffer is also another fear they self-torture themselves, as well as the unknown destiny they are facing and are forced to abandon control over their own life. Of all their fear, anxiety and frustration become their resentment towards reality, these will develop panic attack for all the painful diagnostic procedures and treatments they have to go through constantly, therefore, day by day follows after, stress which causes cardiovascular disease develops another causes of death they may be associating with, because acute stress can possibly aggravate cardiovascular disease. Rozanski, Blumenthal, and Kaplan (1999) note, acute stress can cause constriction of the coronary arteries, arrhythmias in the heartbeat, stimulation of platelet function (which promotes the formation of clots), and increased viscosity of the blood.

Group therapy of CBT with DBT is particular effective for chronic ill patients, because in group they feel comfortable in non-judgmental environment and develops successful therapeutic alliance. Stress can cause a breakdown of psychological defenses between autoimmunity and immunologic incompetence for which patients of this type are mostly suffered from rheumatoid arthritis, thyroid disorders and tumors, for the reason that within the SNS responds to emotions involves enlarging adrenal glands, which in turn releasing glucocorticoids adrenal hormones that triggers shrunken thymus gland and gastric ulcers etc. By using rapport treatment, patients began to interpret their negative automatic and intrusion thoughts spontaneously; this offered authenticating data for studying their physical and mental condition to a greater or lesser degree concern. And these concerns are involved with the depression of the patients which then transited into anxiety, become lack of concentration, continue making nightmare, and are in anhedonia. Cognitive neuroscience investigated that these core symptoms of the disability of both motor and cognitive functions are affected by the low serotonin level, when the neurotransmitters are being dysregulated during the phase of panic anxiety situation, and heart palpitation, muscle tension and apprehension are excited physically. Rapport scale to measure mental and physical symptoms are based principally on crucial acceptance to establish therapeutic relationship.

In CBT acceptance doesn't mean to blindly agree but rather not to be judgmental on the patient's faults. Rapport effort expresses the empathy for and cares about the changes of the patients from masking themselves under a guilt feeling of negative automatic thought threatening life to social goal seeking development. After the patients realized they are accepted they will become expressive to confront their mental stresses to the therapists. By making use of the free association, their mental problems are explained; raw data can be arrived to set for the scale for measuring the components to study the underlying disposition of illness. Cognitive neuroscience uncovers this measure as negative automatic thoughts by threats and fear that changes bodily function,

Part Two

Mindfulness

In the conventional world encompassing with stressful demands for endeavoring in working classes, businessmen and business women, celebrities have to face the media, competitiveness in sports, teachers, young people in school study, and those engaging with high technology to promote skills, as well as health professionals, etc., mindfulness is an essential practice for protecting mental health. Mindfulness in CBT (Cognitive Behavioral Therapy is a congruence practice between mind and physical health. Its techniques include muscle relaxation, deep breathing, exercise training and nutrition program. Why are muscle relaxation and exercise meant so much to our mental health? The discussions here offer every one of you the answers which are able to meet your requirements to build up good body, and sound mental health. Physical exercise means providing "oxygen" to our heart, lung and brain. Heart disease is one of the most fatal illnesses of our life, generally the coronary heart disease which is caused by the blockages in the arteries that supply blood to the heart muscle. Most of the chronic stress client shows severe changes in the walls of blood vessels expose to the development of atherosclerosis which are caused by molecule and endothelin that results coronary artery spasm and myocardial ischaemia, thus exercise benefits the prevention of cardiac events in heart attack. A hormone named the catecholamines serve to modulate the heart rate and initiate the contractions of the cardiac muscle that constitute the heartbeat, as such, skeletal muscles contain extrafusal muscle fibers which provide the force of contraction, during the physical exercise the connective tissues associating with muscles become stronger to withstand the force of contraction, this plays a significant role to recruit strength for proving the entire normal blood circulation to the brain, and heart function. When person exercises, the muscle connecting with the neural pathway of the reticulospinal tract for communication with the subcortical regions, including the amygdala, hypothalamus, and basal ganglia begin to constitute the level of motor integration, and throughout this process our perception is then coded by the parietal lobes for detection of visual information to form learning ability. Physical exercise in a more profound understanding in a way that the muscles and the brain are sharing their roles to restore strength for regulation of normal heart function, at the same time to execute cognitive reasoning in the brain for learning skills. Therefore, physical exercise can prevent Parkinson's disease since the basal ganglia has a direct communication with the motor system. The level of motor integration means the motor systems of the amygdala, hypothalamus, and basal ganglia must be in accurate function to coordinate the contraction and relaxation of the opposing muscle groups such as the back muscle, shoulder and arm involve in anticipating, catching, and holding a thing. This level constitutes transmitting of neurons for continuous communication with the brain to relieve muscle tension while we are under a stressful environment in work or in a sudden panic attack. Relaxation exercise is used for improving blood circulation which is part of the stress management. Cardiovascular exercise includes walking, running, swimming, hiking, and sports training. It is important to note that physical exercise must be performed in good physical conditions, for outdoor physical training such as hiking or climbing, it is important to understand whether the climate is suitable. For children, the exercise intensity should start at low level in accordance with the progress. Some other related methods for mindfulness are systematic desensitization, and assertion training. Self-management programs such as: goals selecting, self-monitoring translating goals into target behaviors', evaluating an action plan, working out a plan for change, audio tape recording of guided relaxation procedures, computer stimulation programs, biofeedback, and hypnosis. In stress, psoriasis and eczema are known to be a related disorder responding to reduction in stress levels, hypnosis alleviates stress and exacerbate psoriasis and eczema. When one is in fear and loneliness, meditation can help our fear transforms into strength, which helps us to seek calm and let go with resilience.

Mindfulness-based stress reduction emphasizes the illnesses occur within the period of anxiety, such as cancer, psoriasis, chronic pain, fibromyalgia, multiple sclerosis, GAD etc. MBSR is focusing on the treatments in both corporate settings of integration medicine with behavioural medicine for health care. Psychological treatment in specific areas such as anxiety imposes hypnosis, meditation, and autogenic training, deep and regular breathing to let go unpleasant thought or images, and alleviate the condition for psoriasis. The components program to manage MBSR consists of relaxation techniques which they are: deep breathing, meditation, visualization, lavender bath, taichi and yoga. Physical therapies includes: body message, reflexology, shiatsu, etc. Cardiovascular exercise includes swimming, jogging, cycling, and aerobics class. Naturopathic diet to stabilize blood sugar levels in order to prevent hypoglycemia from being a stressor. The core therapy for psychological treatment is cognitive therapy for evaluating automatic thoughts which help the clients to act non-judgmental and become problem-solving oriented, devising a plan to ameliorate the situation, profoundly achieving self-acceptance, open-mindedness and commitment to pursue life encountering to benefit a life-long commitment for a successful development of inner-growth that requires a continuous oriented effort of conscious reflection to change from negative emotion to construction one.

There are two kinds of feelings: emotional responses and expression of emotions. These feelings are based on sensory feedback including activities of our muscles and internal organ. As we realize music is the instrument to express and confirm feeling. In classical music, the psychological distance is expressed by musical octaves makeup by sound composition and timbre. For example the subject impression of soft, mellow, broad or full, sharp hollow, nasal and rough or screeching. This complex waveform is played by musical instruments which contain some sound energy at frequencies of 440 Hz, 880 Hz, and 1320 Hz etc. By listening to joyful and encouraging words in a song or music, we are able to replenish our loneliness with positive thoughts by the therapy of musical octaves which express the swift of rhythm to soothe distress and sadness in our mind through the expression sound energy to heal the loneliness and sadness in one's heart. This healing brings us to enter a state to ponder on new thoughts, and a change to survive more optimistically. Arts of painting, calligraphy and music are a form of psychotherapy process, and are to bring a degree of emotional relief which is referred as 'Catharsis'. From these the individual learns to build up his/her inner self to restructure a positive mind.

Part Three

Assessment and Therapy to Alleviate Symptomatology of Anger, Anxiety and Mood Disorders Caused By Failure and Traumatic Events

The triangular related hypotenuse of three types of emotional distress caused by failure and traumatic events are associated with the behaviour of passive aggression (anger), passive avoidance, deflection (anxiety, mood disorder), and lack of drive (depression). Favourite defense mechanism consists of projection to express these three types of mental symptoms such as fear of madness, full-blown panic attack. Unobtrusive measures provide assessments on physical traces. In psychology deflection is a negative force and the inability to focus ourselves to other relevant information when withdrawal of behaviour takes place. When deflection occurs in one's mind, behaviour of avoidance becomes an irresponsible notion. Russell (1978) an existentialist suggests that freedom and responsibility goes in the same direction. He assumes responsibility is a basic condition to change. By using self-actualizing and person-centered therapy (Roger, 1961), the clients can be given an opportunity to develop during the course of cognitive learning to foster great faith in growth. The power of positive thinking insights rational reasoning to which faith and flexible beliefs are the major mechanisms to strive for expectation to succeed, to the task for goal seeking, and to resist distressful forces that may cause depression and anxiety. The gray matter in the hypothalamus controls emotion, it is through this brain mechanism we attain the power to rationalize and control aggressive behaviour, and to reason irritable situations in terms of faith and determination to change for worth seeking intensity. Tension and stress prevail the normal functioning of hormones produce from the hypothalamus to activate the gray matter of the amygdale, in order to provide self-control behaviour against aggression. In cognitive behaviour, the therapeutic processes help depressive patients to percipient faith and flexible beliefs to strive for expectation from positive thoughts

People always wonder whether one can stands alone with positive mind, many fictions and biography describe that loneliness is the best experience to recollect, to visualize each moment of life, to meditate for improving one's mental strength, etc. As a Cognitive Behaviour Therapist, I consider loneliness is the best opportunity to form all mental mechanisms into one integrated system for transformation of new thoughts, new rules to govern the deficits and weakness that defeat our hope. These we give rise to uncover the dark moment of distress in which the Cognitive Psychology termed it as 'Positive mind'. Positive mind does not merely express by performance, it can also be expressed by painting, drawing, handwork and music which are the tools to practice in loneliness. Painting and calligraphy contain imagery for personality structure and muscle training. According to James-Lange theory of emotion, an event in the environment triggers behavioral, autonomic, and endocrine responses. The art of painting and calligraphy therefore attempt to explain these can treat cardiovascular problem. Because several emotion responses are controlled by the autonomic nervous system, the simulated expressions through painting and calligraphy can maintain the activity of the autonomic nervous system in normal function. By practicing these arts transformation of one's soul begins when one's mind is in concentration of the persons fervent piece of art, the flow of gladden joy freshens a person life through the experiencing flare of a galore imagery expression.

Emotional responses and expression of emotions are based on sensory feedback including activities of our muscles and internal organ.

Panic attack respond intense fear, helplessness, and in horror. The symptom involve recurrent and intrusive distressing recollections of the event, image, and thoughts and perception. Patients will be tortured by frightening dreams without recognizable content; they will even hide themselves in the attic or inside a dark closet for hours during a sense of the flashback episode. For more worse they will suffer serious insomnia, loss of appetite, and upset. Social phobia is being afraid to get along with people or be around in the public.

Seven steps to resolve panic attack:

Step 1:   Method: Free Association

Start a written list of possible causes for the first panic.

1. When did your first panic happen?
2. Write down the date in accuracy.
3. What had changed in your life, both good and bad?

Step 2:   Ask the client to top up a list:

1. Try to pinpoint anything you have missed in Step 1 by using the list of events as the table below:

Table 1 – Events which can lead up to initial panic attack.

Tick any event that occurred in 6 months before first panic attack and state the reasons for each.

1. Relationships	2. Health (sleep, illness and other causes)
3. Children	4. Disasters and accidents
5. Finance	6. Work
7. Home	8. Friends & Relations (e.g. close friends have health problems)
9. Crime	10. Anxiety

Was attacked or threatened, or was robbed. What are your weak points to make them take advantage of breaking into your house? Was robbed What are your weak points to Make them take advantage of Breaking into your house? Reasons	Heart rate/ Hypertension

Step 3: Your reaction to the events on the list

1. Review your list. Which is the event you have written down upset and worry you most? Any depression felt after the event happened? Which hour of the day that makes you feel depress generally?

2. If more than a thing does, underline then to remind you later that these might be important root of the causes.

Step 4: Sharing with trustful persons.

1. Share what you have discovered with some trustful persons, friends, family members or even your husband. Speak to them openly and let them understand your fear. By taking openly with trustful persons they may observe what is your weakness and what you have missed to protect yourself in face of danger. Sorting out the missing clues may help you to get your ideas in coordination and regain confidence in yourself.

Step 5: Revising your list

1. Write a new list in sequence of the first important you want to express, then the second most important and so on.

2. Take into account what your friend's opinion in Step 4, what you have underlined in Step 3, and your bravery feelings to cope for what is important.

Step 6: Rational Beliefs

1. Write down opposite each cause of action that you could possibly do to change the situation, help resolve it or make you think positively about it.

2. When we have a next meeting you can talk it over a cry, and express your sadness and anxiety, make simple prayers to console the panic experience, and or initiate legal action if not take already. Draw out a positive conclusion of your ideas.

Step 7:   Taking action
1. Actively take constructive steps to change or carry out some of the actions in Step 6 of your rational beliefs.

Technique to assess the dept of depression which 21 symptoms and attitudes: (1) sadness, (2) pessimism, (3) sense of failure, (4) dissatisfaction, (5) guilt, (6) sense of punishment, (7) self-dislike, (8) self-accusations, (9) suicidal ideation, (140) crying spells, (11) irritability, (12) social withdrawal, (13) indecision, (14) distorted body image, (15) work inhibition, (16) sleep disturbance, (17) tendency, (18) loss of appetite, (19) weight loss, (20) somatic preoccupation, and (21) loss of libido (Beck, 1967).

Family Therapy –

1. Adlerian family therapy
2. Multi-Generational family therapy
3. Human validation process model
4. Experiential/Symbolic family therapy
5. Structural family therapy
6. Strategic family therapy
7. Teleological lens
8. Organization lens
9. Developmental lens
10. Multicultural lens

Ten areas of assessment for multicultural lens:-

1. Membership as an immigrant in a dominant society.
2. Level of economic privilege or poverty.
3. Level of education and process of learning.
4. Ethnicity.
5. Religion.
6. Gender.
7. Age
8. Race, discrimination, and opposition,
   minority versus majority status.
   Regional background..

The Process Lens –

1. The process of communication.
2. Metacommunication.
3. Clarity of process.
4. Face of disruption (internal resources and strengths).
5. Methods to become grounded and rebalanced.
6. New integration with support and practice to achieve a new status quo.
7. Disruption affair to challenge over the case, such as a divorce, or death, hurt and fear, betrayal, disappointment and hopelessness which a therapist has to face with.

A multi-lensed process of family therapy –

1. Forming a relationship.
2. Conducting an assessment.
3. Hypothesizing and sharing meaning.
4. Facilitating change.

Part Four

My Experience Working In the Field Of Learning Difficulty

As chronic stress interfere learning due to hyprofrontality caused by interference with the secretion of dopamine in the prefrontal cortex, learning and the environment are the crucial factors for relationship of changes in behaviour for students who have learning problems, such as students who suffer from chronic illness or who are ADHD learning disorder due to deficits of chromosome 6. The two forms of non-association learning Habituation and Sensitization are helpful to improve learning behaviour for these students. Associative learning of these two forms is classical conditioning which involves learning a relationship between two stimuli, and operant conditioning involves learning a relationship between a stimulus and the organism's behaviour such as neurobiology for learning memory.

Anterograde amnesia is occurred by brain damage in which the person cannot be able to learn new things and new information in the present and future of his or her life, but these patients can remember very well about the events happened in the past before the brain damage. In 1889 Sergie Korsadoff, a Russian physician, discovered that anterograde amnesia is the result of serious chronic alcoholism. The disorder of anterograde amnesia is later given the profound symptom of Korsakoff's syndrome. There are two reasons studied by Sergie Korsakoff for the interrogate amnesia. First, chronic alcoholism causes a deficiency of thiamine (vitamin B_1) by the substantial number of calories from alcohol the patients ingest the patients then lose appetite in taking normal diet (Adams, 1969; Haas, 1988). Second, alcohol prevents intestinal absorption of thiamine and ensuing deficiency taken place in the brain. Why is thiamine important for memory and relational learning? For metabolism reason thiamine carries the intermediate products such as carboxylation of pyruvate in the breakdown of carbohydrates, fats, and amino acid.

Korsakoff's syndrome sometimes occurs in people who have been severely malnourished and have then received intravenous infusions of glucose; the sudden availability of age caused by insufficient of thiamine, then the standard of medical practice is to administer thiamine along with intravenous glucose to serious malnutrition patient. The second symptom of Korsakoff's syndrome is Confabulation. Since the patient couldn't recall or repeat the course of event happened recently, they just simply describe the event factiously rather than telling strictly to others that they can't remember. The term of confabulation can be real or just can be imaginary, these do not mean that the patients are trying to deceive deliberately, but they want to think of another story to replace the lost memory event happened recently in their mind, to avoid letting other people realize that they are suffering from brain damage, and are unable to retrieve new memory or new information. Confabulation can also be explained as a fake behaviour to disguise a normal social life.

Anterograde amnesia is also occurred when the temporal lobe is damaged. Antergrade amnesia may also be the result of being attacked by a trauma to temporal lobe. Amnestic patients are not in one group of chronic alcoholism, or the second group of brain damage at the regions of the bilateral temporal lobe and hippocampus. Because evidence from amnestic subjects suggests that autobiographical knowledge and factual knowledge may involve different brain mechanisms within the temporal lobe. For examples, following trauma to the temporal lobe, some patients will completely lose their ability to recall the previous recent event which happened in the last few minutes, such as dramatic personal events that occurred before the trauma, accidents and deaths in the family. In contrast, their vast stored factual information retained remarkably intact. According to Bechera et al. (1995), the hippocampus and the amygdale play very different roles in the development of emotional and episodic memories. These roles consist of Short-term memory and Long-term memory.

Both short and long-term memories are associated with sensitization changes in synaptic strength at the connections between the sensory and motor neurons. It is explained that presynaptic facilitation in the sensory neuron is thought to occur by means of the GTP – binding protein (Gs), which activates the enzyme adenylyl cyclase, increases the concentration of CAMP in the sensory neurons, long-term memory is represented in multiple regions throughout the nervous system, explicit and implicit memories may involve different neuronal circuits. Explicit memory storage requires the temporal lobe system. Implicit memories involve the cerebellum, amygdale, and for single forms of learning, the specific sensory and motor systems recruited for the task

Methods and treatments

Most children who do not respond to medications do not work successfully in the important areas of academic and social skills (Pelham & Milich, 1991). In addition, the medication after result in unpleasant side effects such as insomnia, drowsiness or irritation and agitation of manner (DuPaul, Anastopolous, Kwasnik, Barkley, & McMurray, 1966). Educational efforts can be broadly categorized into the following behavioral intervention and treatment:

1. Teaching students visual and auditory perception skills are the efforts to directly remediate the underlying basic processing of learning problems.
2. Cognitive behaviour therapy is a treatment to improve cognitive skills through general instruction in listening, comprehension, and memory, expression of needs and reasonable discussion skills, negotiation and rapport combat between children and cognitive behaviour therapist.
3. Targeting the behavioral skills needed to compensate for specific problems the students may have for understanding the way and method of learning, etc.

Visual and auditory perception skills which include three forms of relational learning for perceptual learning, stimulus-response learning and classical conditioning were the techniques provided to treat Petty's irresponsive learning attitude. The technique of perceptual learning is to provide learning to recognize complex visual stimuli involves changes in the visual association cortex; and auditory stimuli involves changes in the auditory association cortex. Stimulus-response learning involves the establishment of connections between circuits related in perception and these involved in movement. The behaviour could be an automatic response such as a defensive reflex to reject difficult vocabularies or difficult questions in an exercise, or it could be a complicated sequence of movements that was learned previously. Stimulus-response learning includes two major categories of learning which psychologists have studied extensively: the classical conditioning and the instrumental conditioning. When a stimulus that initially produces without response several times by unconditional stimulus results a defensive or discursive response (the unconditional response), the first conditional stimulus itself evokes the conditional response. What changes occur in the brain when classical conditioning takes place? In a simple neural model of classical conditioning when 1000Hz tone is presented, for example a perceptual stimulus is presented to visual system, synapse T (transmission) of the neuro transmission is strengthened. Neil Carlson stated that if we present a 1000-Hz tone to an experimental animal and find the animal makes no reaction, it is because the synapse connecting the tone-sensitive neuron with the neuron in the motor system is weak. In other words cognitive behaviour therapy is able to apply stimulus to strengthen synapse T for learning. by classical conditioning. The Hebb rule says that if a synapse repeatedly becomes active at about the same time that the postsynaptic neuron fires, changes will take place in the structure of chemistry of the synapse that will strengthen it (Neil Carlson). How would the Hebb rule apply to our neural circuit for learning? CBT of classical conditioning of 1000-Hz tone reinforces the weak synapse T to become active in the brain that makes the motor neuron fires. After several increments of strengthening, synapse T becomes sufficiently strong to cause the motor neuron to fire by itself and learning has occurred.

In July 2004, through the advertisement a lady called me to provide psychological support to her daughter who had learning difficulty whom I named her Petty in this writing. In the first interview, I examined Petty with differential diagnosis according to the Diagnostic Criteria IV that she had no language disorder, she can express freely in both Eglish and Chinese Language, there was none visual perceptual deficit. Apart from these intelligent skills, she suffered a moderate depression and anxiety, and the overweight problem of Petty was one of the causes for her fatigue in learning behaviour due to insufficient of oxygen supplied to support her balanced physical condition. For such reason, I had to be attentive to the ability she could react to the three forms of relational learning for the starting of the private lesson in the first month, because of her hypertension and fatigue symptoms in learning. Computerized devise for measuring blood pressure was also applied to monitor Petty cardiovascular responses which can be psycho physiological such as blushing; they can also be viewed as vascular responses that are essentially interpersonal. The notion of blood pressure elevation as a form of hidden internal blushing which helps me to make therapeutic use of hypertensive student needs to maintain a comfortable situation at the beginning of therapy. By devising computerized feedback mechanisms that allowed as triturating the magnitude of pressure rises during speech, by using this technique I am in fact both detecting and respecting the social distance defense mechanisms of the student which can avoid her agitation and fatigue in the defensive behaviour for learning. Compulsory as the first start of the private lesson attempts to break through such defenses would only because the student's blood pressure to raise even higher-up to dangerous physiological intolerable levels and becomes more irritable from making learning effort. The reason I applied TP (transpersonal) therapy in my lesson was because TP therapy centers on lowering the cardiovascular component of the fight or flight response in hypertensive dialogue, therefore the lowering of speech for my presentation tone is important for my student to catch and digest the learning. After each hour of the lesson Petty was taught to breathe more deeply, exercise and relaxed her muscles to improve blood circulation.

In an interview with Petty's mother, she described her daughter had social skills and behavioral expressive problems which was the second reason to deprive her learning effort, therefore in my treatment plan I devised a skill on IP interaction for Petty with her family and relatives who loves her most, and she told me her Italian uncle and aunt besides her parents, pay similar loving attention on her, and even her nephew their son, never stops asking for her hug and play time. Petty mother told me my client student had a bad eating habit of rejecting morning breakfast to take before school hour starts. Deprivation from nutritional of serotonin synthesis is the third reason that affected Petty normal behaviour for learning effort. So, in addition to my treatment plan, I decided to provide her a compulsory breakfast taking on each Saturday class for nutritional control of serotonin synthesis. The plasma parameter that couples food composition to brain tryplophan level is the ratio of the plasma tryptophan concentration to the summed concentrations of the neutral amino acid (LNAA) as tyrosine, phenylalanine, and the branched-chain amino acids leucine, isoleucine, and voline (Ferstrom & Wurtman, 1972, 1974; Wurtman, 1974; Wyrtman, Hefli, & Melamed, 1980). This parameter is important because the transport macromolecules within the capillary endothelia comprising the blood-brain barrier that carry circulating typtophan into the brain also transport the other LNAA with the most efficiency, so circulating tryptophan must compete with the other LNAA for transport sites (Pardridge, 1977) to strengthen the synapse T. for learning (Luk, Chan Oi Chee Yvonne). To study the result I used Single-Case (N=1) Experimental Designs., that is the experiment is on the baseline stage to record the individual's behaviour prior to any intervention. To do this I did not offer a breakfast to treat Pearl for serotonin synthesis to study the outcome of the difference with the control. She became hypertensive and fatigue to provide any response for my lesson, after an hour started of the lesson agitation occurred in her behaviour and followed with depression to take further learning performance. That means the nutritional control of serotonin synthesis is crucial for functioning the synthesis of catecholamines and acetylcholamine. Under basal conditions, when a particular catecholaminergic or cholinergic neuron is not firing frequently, it will respond poorly if at all to an increases in available tyrosine (Scally, Ulsan, & Wurtmann, 1977; Fuller & Snoddy; 1982) or choline (BurKamper & Goldberg, 1980).

However, when the neurons are physiologically active, they concurrently become highly responsive to increase in precursor levels, synthesizing and releasing for dopamine, for example, when brain tyrosine levels are raised (Wurtman et al., 1980; Melamed, Hefti, & Wurtman, 1980) and more acetylcholine after choline (Wecker, Dettbarn, & Schmit,

1978) or lecithin (Wurtman, Hirsch, & Growdon, 1977) is eaten. Tyrosine has been reported to help some patients with depression (Gelenberg & Wurtman, 1980).

Methods for learning control in treatment I applied were as follows:-

1. Manipulation holding conditions constant, and balancing. It is essential for observing relationship between stimulus in classical conditioning, operant conditioning and changes of behaviour for learning. The control allows me to make causal inference that the independent variables caused the observed changes in independent variables. Choices for selecting appropriate nutrients to feed into the theoretic action of serotonin 5-HT are the independent variable, that provided the result of changes in behaviour for enhancing the effort of learning (observed changes in independent variables.

2. The techniques I used for holding conditions constant were:

   (i) coaching the student in constant pace with learning in various subjects;
   (ii) illustration of learning attitudes;
   (iii) checking of physical conditions through muscles mobilization, (this is important for offering the subject the condition of time-order relationship to cope her stress when manipulation is used and a subsequent change in learning behaviour is observed. Pulse and

BP monitor equipment was also applied for safety purpose during the stress manipulation experiment;

(iv) illustration of timing and scheduling for learning behaviour to help the student prepared her tests and examinations in due course;

(v) coaching the student cognitive independent variable to make balance between learning effort and failures. The aim is to infer the interaction of cause and effect patterns on behaviour of effort and failures. In my treatment, I must take precautions of taking the risk of running the relationship of being rejected with aggressive response caused by the emotional and fatigue relapsed of the client, and her influenced parents in the process of behavioural change in CBT and within psychological interventions for stimulus-response learning and classical conditioning. Therefore, tasks for elimination of plausible alternatives and unconditional psychological acceptance with empathetic expressions must be maintained to establish a trustful relationship. In order to prevent the risk of ruining a therapeutic trustful relationship, cognitive independent variable becomes a key mechanism for observing the student effort and ability whether she/he can be able to coach her self-alliance learning behaviour with sufficient strength.

Results for Neuropsychology, Cognitive Behavioural Therapy and Psychotherapy –

By observing the student cognitive independent variable I am able to recognize her mental capability condition for Short and Long-term memory within sensitization and habituation changes in synaptic strength at connection between sensory and motor neurons. The student cognitive strength is up to level at scores of 80, but very weak in independent learning attitude since she is lack of social interaction among her peer group since she is the only child of her parents. Psychosocial interaction and Cognitive training are good enough to provide her perception on cause and effect in balancing program to help her to improve her independent learning attitude and judge her own future. Dietary concerns on phosphorylation and adequate food supplements are required for Petty's growth at teenage for strength and matobilism to provide neural circuit for learning.

Regular Frequency for teaching and learning: Luk, Chan Oi Chee Yvonne

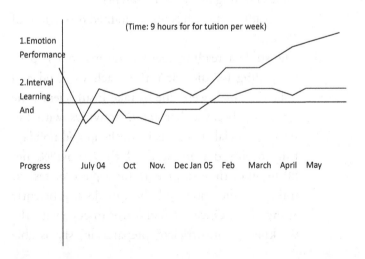

In observing the regular frequency for teaching and learning I applied Psychoeducational Tests as below:

1. The diagnostic battery includes a standard spelling test, written composition, processing and using oral language (daily).
2. The reading subtests of the Woodcock-Johnson Psycho-Educational Battery-Revised, and the Peabody Individual Achievement (daily).
3. Test-Revised are useful in identifying reading disability.
4. A screening projective battery includes picture-story tests, and sentence completion (I used English Literature and Chinese LiteratureEnglish for oral and written exercises to test my student Pearl).

Neuropsychological study on the student client –

1. The student has high intelligence in memory and understanding of the text contents.
2. Her reading effort has not contained distortions of words.
3. The student reading speed is normal but is poor in spelling for dictation after each weekend and holidays which were due to take insufficient time for study because her rapid activities with her relatives' social functions in weekend and holidays fully occupied from study. I then provided her 20 minutes time to prepare for a piece of text or unknown dictation and she can do it efficiently at my place. Once she had learnt to cope with the weakness of insufficient preparation, she is able

to manage the skills of learning and re-exhibits self-esteem.

Differential Diagnoisis –

1. Petty has no language disorder, she can express freely in both English and Chinese Language.
2. There was none visual perceptual deficits.

Mathematics Disorder –

1. Petty has none impairments in four groups of skills: linguistic skills, perceptual skills, mathematical skills, and attentional skills. Her understanding in mathematical terms and to converting written problems into mathematical symbols is good.
2. She has a perfect developmental coordination except she resists long-hours of work on the same topic.

Outcome of the CBT –

Petty has developed patience to take up study through training of emotion daily. Her problem for learning is mainly on emotional and impatience behavioural problems leading to rebellion behaviour which is at the starting of developing Borderline Personality Disorder. I had given her treatment of 10 months for 9 hours per week that required an optimal patient-therapist relationship in psychotherapy and cognition models, as well as nutritional therapy to support her learning effort which she often ignored in the past. Physical training is also included for coaching muscles to cope with emotional training. Sensitization and Habituation both refer to non-association learning for Short-term and Long-term memory, in which of their supporting theory is classical conditioning – a learning relationship between a stimulus and the organism's behaviour. For example, sensitization in synaptic strength at the connections between sensory and motor neurons is the action of serotonin (5-hydroxytryptamine, 5-HT) to recruit the stimulus and retrieve memory for a task. Operant conditioning also involves learning relationship between a stimulus and the organism's behaviour. Unconditioned stimulus is mostly used for Habituation of non-association learning, such as student who is in fatigue. Unconditioned stimulus requires food such as phosphorylation of the substrate proteins of pathway 1 and 2, and the second portion of active zone and the development of new-synaptic connections. The amount of nutrients daily to remain in optimal health condition for protein is approximately 50 to 70 grams, depending on body size, or 12 percent to 20 percent of caloric intake as protein, Co^{2+} channels requires food such as milk, yogurt and cheese to transport biochemical between sensory and motor neurons. Students in fatigue also need coaching on muscles exercise to recycle the gamma motor neurons to enhance associated learning, through nervous system of invertebrates and in simple vertebrate behavioral system. Habituation of spinal reflexes is a good model for studying habituation (AldenSpencer and Richard Thompson).

The latest school report Petty resulted had an average of 80 pass mark for her school mid-term examination, which was a big different from the first one of having an average of 45 for all the subjects she took in the first term examination. Petty mother was very happy and excited to know that Petty has gained a group of friendship in her class with similar learning effort and achieving satisfactory results. Erikson views the age of 12 – 18, the major developmental conflicts of the adolescent years are related to the formation of personal identity in family and in school, if they are being discouraged and failed to cope for positive acceptance in their family, bad school result, and rejection by peer groups, role confusion will result on intimacy versus isolation, this failure may lead to later stage of life on integrity versus despair for which the failure to achieve ego integrity is a feeling of self-disgust, resentment, despair, hopelessness and guilt to experience low self-esteem. Jung pointed out significantly on the importance of constructing primary goals for success that compiles with love, attention and trust in family and peer group as the foundation of achieving individuation, which is the harmonious integration of the conscious and unconscious aspects of personality.

Part Five

Autism

Autism disorder is one of the causes of learning difficulty, it is the impairment in communication, in interests, social interactions, activities, and restricted impairment. Autism with medical conditions is including hypsarhythma, congenital rubella (German measles), tuberous sclerosis, cytomegalovirus and difficulties during pregnancy. Autistic children spend countless hours in stereotyped and ritualistic behaviour such as spinning around in circles, biting nails etc. I had treated children of autistic disorder several years ago, and realize their deficits in learning behaviour are caused by being deprived from parental care in early stage of their life besides the above stated reasons during pregnancy. They are neglected of direct eye contact from their parents and were placed in the cradle in most of the day once they had been fed. The nanny or baby sitter of these kids while their mother are away to work, neglect to maintain a closer connection to care for holding the babies and make eye contact with them regularly when they need emotional pamper during loneliness, because the nanny and baby sitter view themselves as caregivers rather than in a position of having an intimate relationship with the babies as their mother. As the children grow older, they tend to seek attention by performing ritualistic behaviour, rather than having the need to make eye contact with parents to look for help and attention. In this area, I prefer working parents to spend at least an hour to socialize with their children in the evening before bed hour, and to initiate as much as eye contact to their children for caring their inner urge for love and attention, this is an important method to improve their cognitive function. Apart from this reason, neurobiological influences is another reason that causes autism, which autism can be associated with some form of brain damage, it is another form of autism in mental retardation, and has been estimated that between 30% and 75% of the autism display some neurological abnormality as clumsiness, and abnormal posture or gait, but for those who have mental retardation without brain damage are not necessarily with autism. Autism usually has destructive behaviour of self-injury, they jump down from chair onto the floor, they slap themselves during the burst of tantrum, they pull their hair, they hit themselves onto the wall, it is very difficult for them to sit and learn. The most obvious symptom seen in autistic children with brain damage are those having aphasia disorder, a speech disability or having a phenomenon of echolalia, repeating a word or phrase spoken by another person. My treatments for this type of autism is to focus on enhancing to reduce tantrum and self-injury, and to train their skills for learning, training is provided to form communication between parents and children. In April, 1999, I was assigned to treat three autistic children at the age between seven to nine to write a theory and practice for completing my PhD Program of The University Of Southern Queensland, my core training is to grasp hold of their deficit in echolalia, and turned it into strength as a skill to teach them for learning to read vocabularies, in the class, by holding their cheeks facing me with direct eye contact as a technique in stabilizing their emotion for attentional learning, and by repeating my words slowly they followed the phonetic and pronunciation of the vocabularies, as well as the meaning of the word I pointed at the pictures to catch their attention, after reading on the words several times, they were able to read the word by themselves amazingly, a candy or a badge with toy head was offered to these kids when they complete a task for learning successfully, a lunch box was also provided that they were willing to sit down and used a spoon to finish the entire case although some food was spilled on the table and floor, at least they had learn to socialize with other kids in the same group. I applied similar skill to train their memory for learning to recite a phrase after the first step succeeded, and 2 days later they can make dictation. After a week of working hard on the steps to enhance the practice, the autistic children were able to achieve 70 scores for the dictation comparing with the normal students in school.

Cognitive neural science perceives internal representation of a human mind is discriminate between stimulus and response. Perceptual change through childhood for attention learning involves the notion for integration, which is related to child's constructing mental models such as pictures or images, we called this schemata, that this integration is for the role to perform learning in various situations given by perceptual information. When children perceive by monitoring eye movements, search component of visual attention acquires to construct mental models. It is because at 2 months old infant cannot perceive objects as precisely as adults do, but they can make tracking moving stimuli in the periphery of the visual field, their perception totally rely on the internal features of the stimulus excluding the overall pattern. For infant in first month old, it can only perceive the triangle corner by the first contour encountered. From 3 to 4 years old, children perceive object as 2 months old, they begin to rely on internal details of the figure with only an occasional eye movements beyond the contour boundary. From 4 to 5 years old, children begin to make eye-movement excursions toward surrounding contour. A systematic scan of the outer portions of the stimulus with occasional eye movements into the interior or develops at 6 and 7 years old, they start developing the retrieval of perceptual memories of objects and locations. By practice of learning new stimuli object replaced the old object-memory retrieval task. Attention and learning requires the aspect of covert orienting for both direct and information cues. Although memory retrieval has already developed at the age of 7, but children at 11 and 12 years old have to be trained for shifting their attention between information from two visual locations, and between their information retrieval through auditory system, for the visual perceptual memories cannot be separated with the auditory system since the object-memory retrieval task activated the ventral stream in the inferior temporal cortex, while the spatial memory retrieval task activated the dorsal stream in the posterior parietal cortex, both major regions visual association cortex of the inferior temporal cortex and the dorsal stream of the posterior cortex have direct reciprocal connections with the prefrontal cortex, and the ventral stream has connections with the region ventral to this sulcus, this is known as discrimination of orienting filtering for learning and communication (Dr. Yvonne Luk, 2013). Thus, damage to the region or temporary deactivation by cooling the cortex disrupts performance on a variety of delayed matching-to-sample tasks using visual, tactile, or auditory stimuli (Passingham, 1975; Bauer and Fuster, 1976; Shindy, Pasley, and Fuster, 1994; Biodner, Krager, and Fuster, 1996). The perceptual functions of the right hemisphere are in majority of analysis of space and geometrical shapes and forms, which is for identification of information supplying analysis to the sequential stimuli in the left hemisphere to form vocabularies of words for speech production. Therefore, deafness that caused speech disorder is definitely not a diagnosis for aphasia. The measure of sensitivity in discrimination between two stimuli is d' and is affected by the changes in the criterionβ, which d' represents a measure of discrimination similar stimuli, by the fact that discrimination of perceptual functions requires the corresponding of neural circuits in the Broca's area for motor memories to produce muscular movements to articulate words.

Autistic children can be treated by classical response (CR) elicited under certain conditions by a particular stimulus, e.g. they can be taught to take a coin and put it into a container when they are hungry or asking for help. Operant conditioning trains autism children to learn a consequence action for restrained behaviour, and behaves in a way that produces a reward, e.g. the autistic must learn to dress themselves up neatly before a bar of chocolate is given to them as a reward, for those with gait posture they have to be treated with muscle message before provided this self-care training, this will act as recovering their muscle strength to facilitate movement of their limbs. Avoid conditioning can teach autistic children to avoid painful experiences, e.g. placing a candle light beneath their palm for a short while to make them feel the heat of the fire, they would then never try to go near the stove in the kitchen or near the fire place in cold winter to catch fire on their body. Training for communication requires enormous patience which involves imitation and shaping, vocal speech in sign language and devices that have vocal output and can literally help the child. They must be encouraged to play with toys or with peers for their training in behavioural procedures, in order to learn the method to initiate and restore social interaction for forming meaningful friendship. Behavioural procedures are learning skills for developing cognitive function. Medical treatment has not yet been found to cure autism, by using intensive behavioural treatment for communication and skills can improve their cognitive and language disabilities. I insist hectic working parents should sacrifice at least an hour daily after meal for their children to communicate with them not only for understanding their needs, also as a criteria for their children to learn how to master their emotion in the trust with parents because in vice versa emotion serves as a form of communication which resentment makes children feel unloved and unwanted.

Part Six

Facilitation of Will Power

In part one of this book, I mention that physical and psychological health is the crucial drives to manage our positive way to strive for success. Without these variables, we would live with empty mind depriving our freedom to prosper our potential to prosody our worth.

Of all these years of my working experience in psychotherapy, helping my clients to build up optimal level of performance, depression is the biggest problem of destructing success and ongoing effort. It attacks people heart and soul vehemently when a person becomes vulnerable in a helplessness condition following by cognitive dysfunction, for example, during panic attack, repression, low self-esteem, failure in a piece of work. The destruction of will power often happens during recurrent and persistent of negative thoughts marked by anxiety associating with distress, anxiety, and depression that penetrates cognitive function resulting to a neurological insult, as a Applied Psychologist and psychotherapist, it is essential for me to understand if distress is exposing to similar stimuli such as illness, or a constellation of environmental pressures and biological changes in young people affects the clients' behaviour. In these cases I will teach my clients with self-help approach for communication and social skills to reduce and eliminate undesirable maladaptive behaviour on destructive responses. Methods including dispute on old beliefs, situational process to resolve automatic thoughts for making suitable adaptive response and outcome. Imagining yourself taking an escalator to incline or decline onto a selecting location, decline here doesn't mean you are falling backward forever, it's just a situation to readjust yourself to travel to a suitable level you select for your journey to reach the destination, and you have to make your choice to incline again in order to cross over to another side of the journey to arrive at the destination from one building to another. The journey depends on how you make, as human has freedom of choice. Life is the same as taking an escalator or hiking on a mountain, we need perseverance to adapt situational change. In GAD (General Anxiety Disorder) is reflected by the activity in the right hemisphere of the brain, thus encouraging my client to solve the problems by facing fears and frustration is to elicit substantial negative affect and autonomic activity, at the same time instruct them to relief muscle tension that can possibly cause a high level of creatinine to interrupt their cardiac system.

People lacking of will power will also have low self-esteem and devastation used to involve with marriage and family problems, divorce becomes a result to blame one another, get trapped into old patterns of emotional reactivity. During their crises of breaking up, I will encourage my client couples to make trials on supporting one another with personal existence environment and collaboration, e.g. homeostasis family process, and to put emphasis on emotional neutrality and objective on the topics to be discussed for the benefit of one of them recovery from depression, PTSD, panic disorder or OCD. This family therapy stresses crucially on personal connection and conjoint family process to allow couples to learn for cooperation within change in life circumstances under difficult situations. The integration of CBT and psychotherapies consist of the client key focus in understanding significant life change to arrive for "Will Power" to live on with the family, my role in this part is to constrict both the awareness and performance involving new choice in other situations for transference and counter transference to help my clients incline their stepping stones on existential concepts with cognitive approach. As Bugental and Bracke assert that the values and vitality of psychotherapy approach depend on its ability to assist clients in dealing with the source of pain and dissatisfaction in their lives. The reason I used existential theory in most of my psychotherapy is I am able to help them discover new strategies that will guide their individual freedom in each aspect of their daily life to change their belief and situation.

Depression is not something horrible, nor incurable, it is only a kind of emotion problem like all other medical matters that needs attention and care, and rational reasoning for yourself.

- The End -